Love on the Alexander Hamilton

by Ron Overton

Hanging Loose Press

Hanging Loose Press wishes to thank the Literature Program of the National Endowment for the Arts for a grant in support of this project. The author would like to note that many of these poems were written during the period of his NEA Creative Writing Fellowship.

Some of these poems first appeared in the following publications: *Apple, Bird Effort, Cafe Solo, Golden Hill, Graham House Review, Hanging Loose, Happiness Holding Tank, Kansas Quarterly, New, Open Places, Poetry Northwest, Poetry Now, Salmagundi, Shenandoah, Some, Street Press Postcards, Sumac, SunStorm, Three Rivers Poetry Journal* and *Zephyr.*

Cover art and design by Joy Schleh
Layout and design by Zirlin Graphics

Library of Congress Cataloging in Publication Data

Overton, Ron.
      Love on the Alexander Hamilton.

      Poems.
      I. Title.
PS3565.V436L6   1985   811'.54   85-798
ISBN 0-914610-39-2

Published by Hanging Loose Press
231 Wyckoff Street
Brooklyn, New York 11217

Contents

I The Motor Boys Under The Sea

The Motor Boys Under The Sea	9
Miles	10
The Collyer Bros.	11
And	13
American Flyer	15
The Motor Boys In Strange Waters, Or, Lost In A Floating Forest	16
Poem, Ending With A Quote From Roger Vadim	17
Still Life	19
Sharks	20
3 Notes	21
The Death Of Peter Sellers	23

II Getting To Know Your House

Formal Picture Of My Grandfather (1873-1943)	27
First Love	28
An Anecdote	29
Fear Strikes Out	31
Home	32
Testimony On The Axe	35
The Somewhere Else Ghazal	38
Love On The *Alexander Hamilton*	39
Great Disasters	42
The Fathers	44
Getting To Know Your House	45
Letter To A Friend	47
The Infant	50

III The Lone Ranger

Feeding The Stray	53
The Surgeon General Has Determined	54
Postpartum	55
The Reprieve	56
The George Mikan Story	57

The Strong Man   58
Holmes, Unemployed   59
The Lone Ranger   60
2:15   61
The Telephone   62

IV American Light
Why We Came Over   65
Westerns   67
1895   71
Berne, Indiana   73
The Founding Of New England   74
American Light   75
Turning 39 Thinking Of Jackie Jensen   80
School   81
The Weather   82
Seville Ghazal   83
U.S.A. Ghazal   84
Driving: Yes Or No?   85

For Linda, of course

I THE MOTOR BOYS UNDER THE SEA

THE MOTOR BOYS UNDER THE SEA

A strange Sight, as we had learned to expect,
Is followed by A Strange Disappearance.
We kept on.

Until the Fearful Gale.
"In she goes!" cried Ned. "Some blow!" panted Bob.
Only Professor Snodgrass seemed dead to the storm,

Calmly perusing his charts and theories. . . .
Eventually, what was clear was admitted:
The *Hassen* had gone down.

And there was for us no Harbor but The Deep.
A Hammerhead dozing outside the pane,
The Crazed Captain's grin,

The recurrent dream of The Drifting Boat
Wobbling and yearning toward the sun:
All we must endure knowing somewhere ahead

Lies Escape, the Ascent. . . .
We have been In Chains, we have been Entangled,
We have slipped on the air and fallen to here:

Utter Dark. Yet we can see, as clear as America,
The Water Flowers unfolding their spindly arms,
The terrible End of Dr. Klauss,

The surfacing,
The rainbow of spray,
The steady Homecoming in bright air.

MILES

Once in a cushioned theater.
Once in a gymnasium all adamant
of shellac & black lines.
Once in Central Park,
smoke tangling softly in the spots
like a proposition.
If you gave birth to the cool,
you were down to visiting rights.
The mute was out.
Notes opened like switchblades.
"The invisible worm that flies in the night,"
Jack said. Shuffling in the dark
toward the parking lot:
"What the hell is that?"
"Trees."
Trees turning their backs.

THE COLLYER BROS.

1   *The Event*

In 1947 New York gawked,
the doors swung open on 140 tons of junk:
14 pianos 2 cornets 1 bugle
1 phony Stradivarius the jawbone
of a horse stoves and so forth
shotguns walls of print for crushing thieves. . . .
And stashed in the basement of course
their shiny secret:
Langley's Model T.

The dumptrucks whined & spat like drunks,
hauling through the dark of 20 nights.
Our temperate necks were stiff for weeks.

2   *Langley on Homer*

"Homer eats 100 oranges a week—
and is improving."

3   *Homer on Homer*

"I am Homer L. Collyer, lawyer.
I want your name and shield number.
I am not dead.
I am blind and paralyzed."

4   *The Sewing Machine on Langley*

Homer died of course,
despite his clear sense of self.
Starved.
Umbilical Langley (10 feet away)
with the sewing machine
on his tiny chest.

5   *Exposition*

Their father was a gynecologist,
the neighborhood was running down.
So: their world contracted
to sullen gathering.

It has to do with fear.

                    (from an article by Robert Cowley)

AND

1

"We'll fix your wagon," snap the swarthy mobsters
who appear to control the bank.
"The Carioca Club will never open again!"

More trouble. It looks bad for hoofing it.
And after coming all this way!

2

But three chorus girls are dancing on the wing of a biplane,
the band's Latin beat is hot enough to be heard even up there,
they are all in step, and they are all snapping their fingers
precisely and smiling like beauty queens.
"Gee, this is swell," cries the blondest one.

And one falls, the most fiery one, and we gasp,
but even before we are finished she is safe on the wing
of another biplane, one that had to be flying under another
because the pilot was balding, from a drawn-out divorce,
and couldn't take the chance of a bad burn.

3

So she will marry him.

And she does, at the newly refurbished Carioca Club—
everybody getting fresh starts!—
with the band in their black bowties and pasted-down hair
playing a silky number and all the couples dancing dreamily
across the floor, framed by potted palms,
a cool light shining in all of their eyes,
so glad to be back on the ground,
where maracas gossip lazily
and everythig is grand again.

AMERICAN FLYER

Nothing matches.
The dappled vinyl pigs and cows
are fat as the airplanes
which are smaller than the cars.
The billboard is bigger than the station.
No wonder the train has disappeared into the tunnel.
The boy has slipped into the tunnel too,
he is speaking softly to the train,
one eye larger than the other.
The diner's lights are still on.
Small cars drive up to the station.
Men in business suits get out and stare, amazed.
The tracks are gone.

THE MOTOR BOYS IN STRANGE WATERS,
OR, LOST IN A FLOATING FOREST

Ah, this is no easy element:
A confusion of land and water.
It is quiet here at night.

After seven days, we lost our way.
Moreover, we are subject to a plot
Of uncertain authorship.

On the fifteenth day
We absently slew the sacred Manatee.
Since, Bob has fallen ill.

Something here is familiar.
We almost find tongue for it,
Yet silence has us

By the hair.
But for our lovely machines,
This halved world should stun our hearts.

We shall escape.

POEM, ENDING WITH A QUOTE FROM ROGER VADIM

1

She was Slavic alright,
but couldn't contain her joy.

2

She was weeping & naked
but French. So I left.

3

She was weeping and Slavic,
but she was wearing a G-string.

4

He was nude, Slavic & weeping.
Life can be so cruel.

5

She was nude & Slavic
but had stopped weeping
when I got there.

6

She was Ethiopian, full of sympathy
& wore three hats.

7

Enough is enough.
I gave up in the seventh year of my quest.
Still,

8

"A nude Slavic woman weeping,
to me, is irresistibly sexy."

STILL LIFE

The houses to the left are made of brick
And trimmed with white: the houses to the right
Are essentially the same. Each has a white
Door, white trim, and five white slats that stick
Up out of the window box to restrict
The climb of any flower or vine that might
Decide to veer. The roofs are all a light
Gray and of a slant that would predict
A serious spill for anyone who tried
To climb one: it would be best I'm sure to stay
Down on the wide green lawn. A small white cyl-
Inder is what the chimney is, in size
No bigger than a can of beans and made
Of tin. Behind it the sea lies perfectly still.

SHARKS

Hammerhead

Water touches the boat
like a dreaming hand.
He is all green shadow.
In the drowsy prongs of his head
two small fires burn.

He is still as a sunken ship.
The accountant tosses a cigarette,
but he refuses to move.

Mako

He vaults between the sun and us,
then bores back into the sea.
The water is mad beneath him
but accepts him every time.

On the dock, the usual pictures—
Two hooks will barely hold him.

3 NOTES

bilingual

i'm bored
george sanders writes carefully

in english & spanish &
as though no one would believe him

if he said it even if he said it right
but would crack come off it george

skip the movies or try to cheer him up
suggest stamp or coin collecting

to make it credible to hollywood
& to the passionate spanish maid

he kills himself

ambiguous

i didn't know
the first one was
a suicide note
until
3 days later
when he asked me
did you get the suicide note
i was shocked
i thought
he was going
on vacation
carlson said

21

somalingual

the undertaker everyone liked
who inherited the business from his father
& who always had a fresh haircut
& a smile at the door

has no smile in his rooms above the parlor
closer now to heaven
than the floor
has left no note but

the scrawl of his legs
the unattended dead below
grinning
in their bright makeup

THE DEATH OF PETER SELLERS

An airliner stalls overhead, floats noiselessly
to earth.

We rush toward it, limbs jostling in the dark,
then abruptly stop.

Everything is intact. The huge white body hums,
light glows from the ports.

Inside, hundreds are dead.

II GETTING TO KNOW YOUR HOUSE

FORMAL PICTURE OF MY GRANDFATHER (1873-1943)

In the rich brown tones
of old photographs he stands poised
between annoyance & love: year of 1943.
In a month I will be born.

They have dolled him up for this,
but before the shutter can close he
has loosened his tie & unbuttoned his coat.
He is not in front of a church.

The smile you see is allowance made
for the photographer who takes too long.
The wicker chair is perhaps one of the hundred
brought home from auctions: the cap

in his hand the one he tipped
to the world: the mustache the one he's said
to have twirled when he won at checkers.
Why the squint in his eyes?

Perhaps he foresees his death:
more likely, it's just the opposing sun.
His dearest possessions, his cigar & his dog,
are missing from the photograph.

FIRST LOVE

Surprised to find that, in a way,
I'm still faithful to you. This dream for instance
of you standing obliquely against the lockers
in your nurse's whites, like a witness

to what might be murder in the street below,
staring down with eyes blue as Earth.
You offer a Valentine, you take it away.
Thanks. You knew my love of no

& could count on it like a Coke.
We were as complicated as a home run.
Now, because we have become something else,
speech is forbidden. But our glances admit this much:

we have settled for something less. We had to.
We know that. The goddamn sages wrote it even in
flung textbooks: & we would scream & lunge
into the bright pool & would not hear.

AN ANECDOTE

1

I drive north
to visit my in-laws.
Past Worcester, reaching into my shaving kit
for a Valium, I cut my thumb
on a razor blade.
The cut bleeds profusely.

2

I stop under a streetlight
in Hubbardston
& bandage it.

3

They say, "It's about time!"
To excuse myself & to shock them
I offer my dripping thumb.

4

They become solicitous,
so I minimize it.

5

My wife reads me "Cut," by Sylvia Plath.

6

It continues to bleed beneath the bandage
all that night.

FEAR STRIKES OUT

I mashed my finger & heard it
shriek like an ump along the bone,
& that was the first time.
Then other things. How a curve whispers
loverlike as it floats toward you waiting.
How the lines were not truly straight,
yet they went by them. How much
the moony ballface was my father's face,
yet when I got good wood on him how
good that felt. Along the bone.

O it never struck out.

HOME

For Robert Hassinger (1943-1968)

For years now you have been dying,
disappearing,
slowly slipping out of sight
like the man overboard
as the ship plows indifferently on.

Only this stays.
A certain morning memory of you,
without theatrics, without knowledge of me,
standing before the room's sole window,
tall & full of homesickness for Ohio,
staring out at first light breaking
on New York's poorest county—
Filmore's botched farms looming from the dark,
clarifying,
as a landscape rises from the developing pan,

the dim fields veined with snow,
a branch slipping in the wind.

                  *   *   *

I think of all winter mornings like that,
coming to our lives:
confused within strange walls & doors,
the distant spill of small voices,
flush of sinks & toilets,

the slur of light beneath the door.
And can sometimes joy in such strangeness.
Or, it is like the suck of undertow,
a black tide
whelming over us.

*   *   *

You, who talked of Savonarola & Rimbaud's hat.
You, who loved the complications of Bach
     more than the complications of women.
You, who chose the fevered rump of Wesley
     over Calvin's parlor grin.

Your parents send me this Xeroxed missionary face
     still full of Armenian sorrow,
     which explains nothing.

I can't drive home.

*   *   *

My first reaction surprised me.
I sat down & thought about your dying:
I thought of "Lycidas,"
now suddenly felt the shepherd's glib faith rise from books,
from the thin hands of explicators

and understood the real ache of the holy,
their restlessness, until in death they are calmed.
Gone home!
For a moment, I went crazy with joy
for you.

*   *   *

In the last dream I had
of you, very close to your death by water
& long before I knew of it,
you held a delicate shape in your hands,
a small body of dust & light
which shook itself, then flew out & up,
loosened to the glittering air.

Later, an angel with a face like a mole or rat
& acting very officiously
came down & put a pencil in your hand.
But you refused it, pointing at him & whispering,
Don't talk about it. Don't talk.
And fell away from him with a physical grace
you prayed nightly for.

Fell away like a drowning man.

TESTIMONY ON THE AXE

"a book should serve as the axe
for the frozen sea within us"
—Kafka

1

I hacked
then put my ear down

through the jagged hole
joplin rags
the clinking of glasses

frankly
I expected more

2

I will use it
I will use it soon

but I keep feeling
this finger tap my shoulder
I turn & no one is there
nothing
the empty blue lawns

I will use it when this stops

3

I sold it
a tough choice sure
but at the moment
I'd rather have the cash

35

4

I hung it carefully
above my workbench

daily of course
I polish the handle's sweet wood
I refine the blade's fine edge
I brighten its flank to a mirror

perfectly reflecting my face

5

I hacked all winter
seven days a week sir
not a crack

simply couldn't get through
after I quit
spring did it in a day

6

I broke open the sea
am sailing upon it
tacking clear as any antony
through his love's summer

& am unhappy

I've lost the axe
& winter will surely return

7

what sea?

8

I used it
& nothing happened

there is a fine slip of blood
on the blade edge
warm to my thumb
I have no idea where it came from
no idea

9

I will never use it
I love the cold

THE SOMEWHERE ELSE GHAZAL

Everyone is writing a novel, a life.
You come to me now with exposition.

As a kid, all year I lived for Christmas, all week
the weekend, all day for recess. Some kid.

Anarchist Huck, his wistful river dream of a life
without women, the drift always to a better place.

Hockey is the most poetic game of all—
there's no bench, no fatboys, everybody plays!

We watch the powdery, fluted lawn. You talk
of sudden leisure, snowmen. I see skids, wrecks.

LOVE ON THE *ALEXANDER HAMILTON*

For Katherine, wherever

We sit on the top deck,
because there are no parents here
& because we can watch the city lights wink on
in the dollhouses along the shore
& imagine the rich lives inside:
he's home from the game with three home runs,
she's lost in a jigsaw of diamonds & furs,
after a crazy kiss we almost see,
they're off to the show in a Jaguar
as dark as the speech of her eyes.
My heart vaults & rams
like the pistons of the *ALEXANDER HAMILTON*.

And then the usher, with his flashlight.

                    *   *   *

HAPPY JACK WARREN INVITES YOU
TO A MOONLITE CRUISE UP THE SCENIC HUDSON
SPECIAL MUSIC! INSPIRING TESTIMONIES!
AND THE WORD OF GOD PREACHED
WITHOUT COMPROMISE! PRAISE THE LORD!
BRING YOUR OWN BOX SUPPER
NO ALCOHOLIC BEVERAGES WILL BE SOLD
OR ALLOWED ON BOARD

                    *   *   *

Under the drab hymnal we secretly
hold hands: half ritual
& half not.
Our new bodies barely touch.

39

Her breasts are small & white
beneath the cotton frock.
Lord, her hair falls to her shoulders so carelessly:
it is the color of straw.

*   *   *

How were we to know
   he was the Federalist who yearned
   for a national bank?
Or that he laughed like a chemist
   when the Gypsy hissed, *Beware of Burr!*
How were we to know he would stop like someone
   lost in the past, pull on his finé pipe & intone:
      What's good for Colonial Carriage
      is surely good for the Country.

My lost love, he sounds like a prig.
He sounds responsible for the oil & cups & plastic spoons
   floating by his ship.
He sounds like the reasonable father
   of an ungovernable son.
Perhaps he could never forgive
   his father's childish sin.
Perhaps he could never forgive himself,
   issue of flesh & mounted flesh.
Perhaps he couldn't stand it, being here.

*   *   *

"Just As I Am," throbbing with contrition,
again & again as
the *ALEXANDER HAMILTON* shudders home against its pier:

40

not like it was afraid
it had stayed out too late with the flapper moon:
but like a huge, indifferent machine
hammering
the dead salt air.

GREAT DISASTERS

the andrea doria sleepily
rolls over on its side
& slips into something more comfortable

the atlantic for example
then sleepily again
this time in extra slow motion

my high school reunion is being held
at the andrea doria lodge &
I don't want to go

watching the newsreel with
my wife wild accusations are hurled
back & forth

haggard faces wrapped in blankets
question the crew's valor
women & children first oh sure

watching the andrea doria roll over
& disappear as slowly
as a decade or two slips under

of graduate stipends volvos neighbors
your basic collisions
& lifeboats

we'll be back next week
the announcer sleepily promises
with more great disasters

the andrea doria laboring now
this is the fifth or sixth time
do something

I say to my wife
something did she says &
I don't want to go

THE FATHERS

Jimmy Piersall of the Red Sox
in the Fifties sprayed
home plate with a water-gun
like I smuggled to school.
I saw it.
Later I saw the movie explain
that he had trouble with his father,
Karl Malden.
You could also see him jawing
with the umps like a mad squirrel,
hopping in and out of the box.
"Why doesn't he just hit?"
I asked my father.

Nothing.

We asked our fathers then,
and they wouldn't say.

GETTING TO KNOW YOUR HOUSE

Sitting

Have you sat in every chair in your house?
Have you sat in the dark in every chair of your house?

Fidelity

Do you glance at other houses out of the corner of your eye?

Hats

As a courtesy, do you take your bowler off in your house?

Sleeping

Have you slept in every room of your house?
Have you had the falling dream in every room of your house?

Plumbing

Do you understand plumbing?

History

Climbing the stairs, do you ever meet a younger you
    coming down?
In this dark way, have you also slipped past previous owners?

The House in Space

When the oil burner goes, does the house seem to be
    motoring through space?
When it stops, does the house come to rest?

At Sea

When you wake in the night, does the house seem to have
    pulled up anchor, to be adrift?

Smoking

When you smoke your pipe, does the house fall asleep?

Death

Have you considered your house living on, after you?

LETTER TO A FRIEND

for Brian Lyke, going on the road

Summer yellow, leaves opening out.
Freshening.
That is to say:
Yes, I understand.
On the move again, the push
to find another place.
There is a grove of pine
in my mind too,
where the sunlight swerves
inward, like a knife,
lighting
a swath of forest floor.
God's movie.
It still confuses me,
I'm loath to speak of it.
But we burn for this, yes—
a place
to turn our questions over & over,
like eggs
in the drifter's skillet.

     *   *   *

I would spell out the virtues
of staying in one place for you,
but they're mostly dreams
of travel.
Tell me:

on the move do you dream
of settling peacefully
in one place?

47

*   *   *

I think often of the car-wreck
you stumbled on, heading home,
alone,
in the chill fix of last winter—
the weight of that stranger
on your living hands,
how did it feel?
Unlucky boy!
Much heavier no doubt
than our best theologies.
His deserted skin,
his soul unfurled like a scarf . . . .

Back at seminary,
was his weight lifted?
Or did your hands drop
to the abstract table,
full of death?

*   *   *

I had a carnal dream,
Father Brian.
We were in a bus terminal
with a lot of girls.
So we agree to collaborate,
pick up a few,

& the first four we ask say yes,
sure, glad to . . . .
Then disappear, giggling;
huddle;
then reappear, ready for us,
though not as you might expect—
transformed, luminous—

but very young & mortal girls.
Eager for fleshly plums.

I took the round one,
aglow with lust, much in love,
& you swept the other three away,
religiously,
zealot of the body—

Ah, lucky boys!
Down the hallway I could hear
your carnal laugh booming so loud

it woke me up.

* * *

As a kid,
I always swam underwater.
Which makes me religious, I guess.

Even then, my hunch was God wasn't
in the sky
but down below,
among the salty particulars.
Let us commune here, under the sea.

He is silent,
so that we may talk.

THE INFANT

for Ned

One warm evening:
a waxy light in the west,
a yelp like a thumb
slammed in the door. Then this
in our house.
We have warned the sleepy town,
we have notified science.
It watches us.

It is a turtle swimming away.
A crab stroking for sand.
It loafs in a stab of sunlight
and will not talk.
And will not.

It is a kind of sloth perhaps,
at night we have poked it.
Some sort of featherless dog . . . .

Across the room, I am lonely.
My heart ticks like a pocket watch.
The street shines in the rain.
Give me its hands.

Walk.
Speak.

III THE LONE RANGER

FEEDING THE STRAY

Who
among us at
one time or another
has not found
a strange cat
on the doorstep one
snowy morning? His
sides almost touch,
his eyes are sunken—
in short,
he may be starving.

Give him first
a drink of warm, sweetened tea.
Let him rest and grow drowsy.
In an hour or two,
give him warm milk
or broth to lap.

You cannot hurry
a starving stray
into good condition.
It takes time.

(Found: Cat Care Manual)

THE SURGEON GENERAL HAS DETERMINED

brown eyes & a gentle, sloping nose.
His is not a handsome face,
& perhaps for this reason he has striven
to become the most admired surgeon.

He is concerned about my smoking,
& he says so in no uncertain terms.
"SMOKING IS DANGEROUS TO YOUR HEALTH," he will snap.
He slips his pink gloved arm into my lungs

& like a magician withdraws three broken blossoms.
"See!" he says with more sorrow than triumph,
"What did I tell you?"
Later, as darkness steals across the lawn,

he whispers, "It is not too late."
He absently touches the hilt of his sword,
he dabbles with the brim of his General's hat.
"But it is late, young man. It is very late."

POSTPARTUM

I'm tired
I'm tired of seeing the end
in everything I see today
sick of assurance
the serene white smocks of doctors
technicians

what forest was I in last night
maybe vermont
a finger tracing veinlike roads
on a map
the body of a high school buddy
parceled up
neatly packaged & laid out
his rosy blood in a cider bottle
where his heart would be
his genitals boxed
& discreetly wrapped in brown paper
his bones bound in two stiff bundles
sheathed in clear plastic
the cordovans there at the foot of the cot
formal & composed
the notebook in place of
his missing head in it
his last scrawl
                    blondes
blondes were always my weakness they

THE REPRIEVE

I first felt the brightness
shining against my lids.
Then I saw the snow.
I woke like a boy in a new room,
swelling toward excitement
as he puts aside the warm quilt.
Or as a lover wakes
to his love's white body—
love, overnight,
has turned the world strange.
Or as the outlaw wakes, relieved,
knowing there are no tracks.
He'll hole up in this town all winter,
he'll joke with the townspeople,
buy them a round of drinks and
walk all over the merciful snow.
He'll go straight.

THE GEORGE MIKAN STORY

I wore glasses & passed off.
Never behind my back. Hell,
we were happy with black sneakers then.
The only thing that was white
was us. Whenever
I messed up I jotted why down.
GEORGE, TWO HANDS FOR THE SET. FLEX KNEES.
And I licked it after practice.
No more. Hell, they drive off singing
in red cars now.

THE STRONG MAN

"Thought staggers through each page like one poisoned."
—Fitz-James O'Brien, on Melville's *Pierre*

My body was in perfect health . . . .
I rang the bell at the Newton Fair.

Now my fingers bang like hammers,
there's a fireball in my belly's black hold.

I lug from room to room, anvil huge.
I want to be found.

A spider, careful as a doctor, spreads himself
on the globe of my eye:

he puts the pain in.
I keep turning, expecting someone, you—

but the room is full of my body
lurching beneath me.

HOLMES, UNEMPLOYED

The pocked forearm,
the pale fingers
worrying a small glass egg . . . .

This gift & no task.
The syringe, the violin.
The days lined up like stones.

THE LONE RANGER

Tonto is embarrassed
to find that a rabbit in the underbrush
has made him jump.

When The Lone Ranger laughs,
Tonto answers, "At least me ready
for trouble."

"Yes, and I am a truly lonely man,"
The Lone Ranger broods. "You, Tonto,
know this best."

2:15

Rubber on cement?
Or cats screaming sex
in the junked Fords out back?

I've come home to find
the friendly tom has lost an eye—
a gold lamp now a grave,
pink as a tongue.

The phone rings once and stops.

the telephone

hello is bartholomew there
no
I think you have the wrong number
oh ok
just tell him that joanie called

IV AMERICAN LIGHT

WHY WE CAME OVER

1

We stop by a virgin
stand of pine by a man-made lake.
It's New Jersey, this land is our land!
Listen . . . .
From the trees comes a ratcheting,
as of a tinny fowl.

All That Wee Here Fynde Is Strange.

2

Yes, we've come from Europe.
We'd been dodging puddles
left by a delicate Old World rain,
in the sallow light we were zig-zagging down
the cobbled streets too narrow for automobiles when,
as in a Musical, three Lovelies
took our tendered arms
& danced us all the way to here, America,
New Jersey,
where we've stopped to rest.

3

God bless Ginger Rogers
& her husband Fred Astaire.

4

The lake is vast & frozen.
Out of the wilderness
applause flushes like quail.
A Packard glides by.

We quickly bow,
we follow it: West.

WESTERNS

1 *Indian Un-horsed!*

The Indians were wonderful
bareback riders—
but the superior weapons
of our Western Pioneers
over-came the native skill and cunning
of the red savages.

Here we see an Indian
shot right off his wild horse.

2 *Ambush!*

The lonely pioneer
was plodding his lonesome way
along the floor of the Canyon,
when the sudden sound
of a rolling pebble
caused him to wheel around.
        There
on top of the cliff
hostile Indians lay in ambush.

The white man close up shot twice
and two red-skins bit the dust!

3 *Doe-Wah-Jack*

A very hardy Indian was Doe-Wah-Jack
and renowned for his fortitude.

In praying to the Great Spirit
he would go as long as four days,
without eating,
or drinking
or sleeping.

4 *Ma-Ta-He-Hah*

They called him "Old Bear"
because he was the mystery medicine man
of the Mandan tribe.

All herbs in the forest were known to him,
and many a baby Indian's stomach trouble
did he cure with his rhubarb roots
and sulphur solutions.

5 *Geronimo*

Before this Apache war lord
was finally captured by the Federal troops
and put in prison, many
were the bloody, vicious raids he made
in New Mexico and Arizona.

He was captured once before by General Cook,
but cunningly managed to escape.

Not so lucky the second time, he
languished in prison until the end of his days.

6 *Sho-Me-Cos-Se*

Sho-Me-Cos-Se ("Wolf" to you)
was a big chief of the Konza tribe.

"Wolf" was a handsome man,
as you can see from his picture,
and was admired and much sought after
by all the squaws
of the Konza tribe.

7 *Cowboy Whoopee*

"Whoopee" now a word in common use
in the English language, was first originated
on the Western Ranch by the cowboy who
used the word "Whoopee" in rounding up the cattle
or wild horses.

Cowboys not only work hard
but also play hard.

Cowboys are apt to call any form of amusement
"Making Whoopee."

"The red-skins are coming" cried
the galloping, warning horseman! Immediately
all the settlers' families hitched up their horses
and rushed for the safety of the neighboring stockade,
where guns and gunpowder were stored.

Behind the sturdy log walls of the stockade
the hardy settlers, men firing and women loading
the guns, fought off the Indians—

and were saved by the Stockade!

(Found: trading cards, c. 1950)

1895

The Sunday School Picnic

No half-way measures
for Mrs. W.B. Jaynes, who at the Sunday School picnic

surprised Mr. Jaynes by an exhibition of swimming,
having learned the art while stopping at Shelter Island.

She overtaxed her strength & the result was
a very white face nestling among pillows

for three long days.
Too ill to speak aloud, a friend calling upon her

found her surrounded by advertisements of bicycles,
planning new recreation which if overdone

will send her on a journey whose end
cannot be attained by a bicycle in this age.

The Lawn Party

Mrs. W. B. Jaynes gave a lawn party July 4th.
The lawn & piazza were illuminated by Chinese lanterns.
Each croquet player was furnished with a shining new lantern.
Late in the evening there was a display of fireworks.
Ice cream of the hostess' own make was served.
The guests were Mr. & Mrs. Carigan,

> Mr. & Mrs. Drew, of Brooklyn,
> Miss Addie Edwards,
> Misses Aida & Fannie Darling,
> Alanson Blydenburgh & others.

The Christmas Festival

The M. E. Sunday School held its Christmas festival
in Music Hall last Tuesday evening.
The platform was tastily decorated & all the exercises
appropriate.
There were two heavily laden, sparkling Christmas trees.
The principal piece on the program was "The Quarrel of
the Flowers," in which Mrs. W.B. Jaynes attired in pink
satin, with a coronet of roses, represented a rose.
Miss May Batchelor in crimson silk personated a fuchsia,
while the other young ladies in white dresses & sashes
the color of the flower each represented, made a beautiful
& harmonious blending of colors.
Alfred Brush in a white costume, with a hat two feet high,
impersonated "Winter."
The march in the play was perfectly done & called forth
loud applause.
The tableau "Christmas Eve" was a beautiful one.
After each member of the Sunday School had received their gift,
it was found that the generous Methodists had provided
for every child in the audience as well.
Rev. Mr. Morehouse, the greatly beloved pastor, was presented
with a rattan easy chair, which all present hoped
he might live many years to fill.

(Found: Smithtown, NY newspaper, c. 1895)

BERNE, INDIANA

Brice Lehman, 10, son
of Mr. & Mrs. Orlando Lehman of this city

was slightly injured Sunday
when attacked by an enraged sow

on the Doyle Lehman farm just
east of Berne. Brice was bruised

but was able to go to Bible School
this morning. He was playing

with Kevin Lehman (son
of Mr & Mrs Doyle Lehman) on

the Lehman farm, & picked up
a small pig. As pigs do,

the animal squealed
& the mother of the little porker

did not like it, came rushing
at Brice & knocked him down.

He was not bitten
& the local doctor could

not find anything wrong with Brice
except he had a few bruises.

(Found: *Berne Witness*)

THE FOUNDING OF NEW ENGLAND

Just a note to tell you
we missed you today at The Old Mill.

Granny was disappointed
you didn't make it.

We all had turkey—
except Robert, he had meatballs.

His old girlfriend, Diane Hoad,
was checking coats.

AMERICAN LIGHT

Homage to Hopper

1

Sunday,
and no one is up yet
to take advantage
of the grey solitude of sidewalks.
Only the monuments of morning stand:
the hydrant's sturdy thumb,
the barber's patriotic pole.

This is the quiet
of shadow
laying itself down upon stone.

2

How bored the usherette is.
She has seen this picture so many times,
the gunshots slip by like gossip
in the street below,
her heart
hangs heavy as the dark red curtains
kept from the sun.
Her life feels like cigar smoke today,
vague and acrid,
not like the rain of gold light
that must be outside.

3

If you go far enough north,
and drive deep enough into summer,
you can be as clear and central
as the lighthouse at noon.
The lawn knows its place.
The houses huddle around for advice.
The sea keeping its distance,
respectful stranger.

4

You take a train from New York City
to New Mexico—everything new!

After days of rain, the sun.
You go outside and paint
the locomotive that brought you here.

5

The trusses and corsets stay up all night,
talking of the Dodgers,
of city life in general—
of how some must serve by waiting.
They are waiting,
our starched apparatus,
upright in the stale Drug Store air,

in the contesting light.

6

Dusk, and the pines begin to sway
like the adjacent sea.
The gas pumps glow.
The attendant waits, rubbing the salt
from his calm blue eyes.
Later, if no one stops,
he will walk deep into the woods
for the first time.

7

The Captain's clapboard house is less wood
than a privacy of weather and light.
Perhaps this is why no one is at home.
They have gone to the carnival no doubt,
spinning in the cluttered air,
taking chances—

8

Is there time for a walk?
Sure, why not.

   the green of the leaves
   like the green
   of certain translucent insects

9

She has slept late.
It is allowed on her day off.
And taken off all fashion,
stripped herself of the city,
to be naked in the blonde light
of nearly noon.

10

The report must be ready by 9 o'clock.
Mary holds a slack attention over by the files,
remembering Indiana;
he bows his head at the desk,
reckoning in his own shadow
so much gained and so much lost . . . .
His hair is thinning.

The foolish laughter in the street,
and winter coming on.

11

The wide window is like a movie screen.
We see only half of the car, a mannequin Buick.
The hills flat and regular,
like the dreamt backs of whales.

But this is the desert.
And she is no starlet.

12

There is nothing in the city
like the solitude of these hulls
rolled on their sides,
in dusky light.

They are the Elect.

TURNING 39 THINKING OF JACKIE JENSEN

jackie jensen is dead at 55
which is now the national speed limit
jackie jensen came up with the yankees
but had his best years with the red sox
jackie jensen hit the highest infield pop-up
I ever saw in my life
in a double-header at yankeee stadium
as jackie jensen waited for the ball to come down
you could see his muscles waiting
jackie jensen was an all-american fullback
but he chose the national pastime instead
jackie jensen was an all-american guy
with classic blond good looks
but jackie jensen had an abbreviated career
because he was afraid of flying
you could see his muscles from the upper deck
but he wouldn't get on a goddamn airplane
so he was left behind in the fifties
in high school I got a jackie jensen glove
and I still have it the "personal model"
though my career has been abbreviated by time
all things that happen happen forever
if you were on a star about 25 light years away
you could see jackie jensen still popping up
if you wanted to
jackie jensen out of time
jackie jensen flying
can you see your pop-up climbing higher and higher
past stars bright as night games
toward you in heaven

SCHOOL

Adora is missing.
Juanita is looking for a light.
Arlene tears her story up.
No one pays attention.

Beautiful Juanita is grown up,
she wishes to marry. Attention
please. Who is missing?
The day withholds its light.

Teri pays no attention.
Tanya, asleep, has given up.
Maria turns off the light.
Where is Adora? Missing.

Juanita is looking for a light.
She wishes to marry. Attention
is not possible. Maria is missing.
Adora turns the red radio up.

THE WEATHER

the magician, the engineer & the elegant
fell asleep on the long trip to Rochester near
Will Durant, Mabel Mercer, Willie Mays, George
formerly employed by the Pentagon, a reliable
blue violets, succulents, & various yellow
suggesting all non-productive citizens re-
house & grab yourself a bird while you
which simply wasn't in the cards this time.
-ingly tired, her eyes red and puffy, so that
from his aircraft, landing in a cornfield
World Series, making this the first time
cheese, paprika, fresh (not canned) mushrooms
the mysterious 18-minute gap, which has never been
flat-chested? Just pick up your phone &
no genius but simply the first to do it.
turning to a light, powdery snow this afternoon.

SEVILLE GHAZAL

The Cathedral's pillars are pocked, massive,
petrified—Inquisition's absolute stone.

Under the desert heat, under the sun's scald,
in a shady bistro, beer so cold my tongue aches!

High Mass: glint of gold, red satin, wine
that should be blood, old beat-up Latin promises.

Watts smolders, Newark burns, Detroit burns—
the New World shatters like a lamp.

Cervantes repented here. And Columbus it's said
sleeps, heart mended, in this gaudy box.

U.S.A. GHAZAL

He eats glass, drinks crankcase oil, gasoline,
sets himself on fire. He's Nixon's dream consumer.

Bored with 'Nam, Blacks, ABM, let's all believe in
the alliterative bullshit of P.R. men, presidents.

She leans by her canvasses, body-stockinged, lisping
for the media her obsessive interest in violence.

The New Breed linebacker hunts the enemy like the old,
but in bellbottoms now, tie-dyed, & radical curls.

By the speech of Ord Falls I imagine new waters—
the inevitable dam, the flood, the silence mistaken for peace.

DRIVING: YES OR NO?

for Robert Hershon

1   *Schools*

E-Z Auto School   *Women instructors available*
Wally's Auto School   *No embarrassing signs or legends*
Safe 'N' Sound Driving School   *Defensive driving emphasized*
Prudential Driving, Inc.   *We specialize in the nervous*
Carl Jung Driving School   *Symbolic driving*
Ingmar Bergman Auto School   *We specialize in the nervous*
Esalen Auto Institute   *Flow-driving, self-directed*

2   *The First Time*

In a shattering of sunshine
it hauls you away and you hold on
like in *The Old Man and the Sea.*
You will perhaps recall forgotten formulas:
something about Mass, something about Velocity.
You will perhaps recall Mitzi Gaynor.
This goddamn thing is big, you think,
and goes on its own.
You almost stop it.
Someone empties the trash.
It goes.
You grin.
You hurt your teeth.
It goes again.
Someone waves from a bus.
You stop it.
It starts to stop.
It stops.

You get out and walk around it,
running one finger slowly along its flank,
appraising it.

3   *Sociology of The Automobile*

Here in the country,
the country isn't here anymore.
So no one went out for football.
Everyone pumped gas for the eventual 'Vette.
(Fred Hosage got one and got so excited
he hit a telephone pole and it melted.)
There was also the Merc', the '57 Chevy, the T-Bird.
And you didn't drive them, you graduated
and went to them, attended them like Harvard.
What you learned you could learn without a car, sure,
and what they did for you you could do for yourself,
if you had a street.
But here in the country,
one place isn't right next to the next place.
So the car happens.

4   *Pros*

There is the sky-as-blue-as-a shirt driving,
    with the elbow out the window and the Stanley Brothers
    on the radio,
there is the famous making out with women or anything
    at the drive-in or anywhere,
there is the picking up of hitchhikers who will hum you a tune
    or tell you funny anecdotes about Arthur Miller,
there is the spitting out the window and yelling out
    the window,
there is the pressing of the small levers that make things
    inside change with a feathery sigh,

there is the song of the radial as it loves the bridge,
    the ballad of the news on long trips through the night,
there is the smooth merging with red taillights at dusk,
there is the impulsive stop at the scenic overlook, thinking
    so this is what it all has been leading to,
    this is the end of my driving,
there is the *deja vu* of sitting in your car alone at dawn,
    knowing you have felt this,
    the knowing you have been here before.

5   *Cons*

You will hit things and be hit by things.
You will mysteriously stop under an overpass in Hartford,
    Connecticut.
You will sense certain friends drawing away.
You will have to rotate your tires.
You will have to pretend to understand the florid
    explanations of repairmen.
You will have to relegate your distrust of them to a small
    corner of your life or suffer endless distraction.
You will slam your thumb in the door and hurt your hands.
You will be strangled and raped by hitchhikers.
You will be shortchanged and insulted by sullen attendants
    forced to work the swing shift.
You will slip into sleep at the wheel and imagine you are
    at sea, rising and falling across New Jersey,
you will fall asleep and even dream,
you will wake and not know how you got this far,
    or where, in the world, you are.